EXPLORE THE UNITED STATES

OKLAHOMA

Julie Murray

Big Buddy Books

An Imprint of Abdo Publishing
abdobooks.com

abdobooks.com

Published by Abdo Publishing, a division of ABDO, PO Box 398166, Minneapolis, Minnesota 55439. Copyright © 2020 by Abdo Consulting Group, Inc. International copyrights reserved in all countries. No part of this book may be reproduced in any form without written permission from the publisher. Big Buddy Books™ is a trademark and logo of Abdo Publishing.

Printed in the United States of America, North Mankato, Minnesota
102019
012020

Design: Aruna Rangarajan, Mighty Media, Inc.
Production: Mighty Media, Inc.
Editor: Liz Salzmann

Cover Photograph: Shutterstock Images
Interior Photographs: Albert Pena/AP Images, p. 29 (top left); AlizadaStudios/iStockphoto, p. 29; Anonymous/AP Images, p. 28 (bottom); AP Images, p. 21; BrianLasenby/iStockphoto, p. 30 (bottom); codyphotography/iStockphoto, pp. 4, 5; Davel5957/iStockphoto, p. 9 (top right); ERIC DRAPER/AP Images, p. 27 (bottom); jay goebel/Alamy Stock Photo/Alamy Photo, p. 29 (bottom left); Jerry Willis/AP Images, p. 28 (middle); Joe_Potato/iStockphoto, p. 30 (middle); Library of Congress, p. 22; lydiabilby/iStockphoto, p. 11 (inset); Marine2844/iStockphoto, pp. 14, 15; NASA, p. 20; raksyBH/iStockphoto, pp. 10, 11; Richard McMillin/iStockphoto, p. 24 (inset); Shutterstock Images, pp. 4 (state seal), 6, 7, 9, 13, 16, 17, 18, 19, 23, 26, 27, 28, 30; Tiago_Fernandez/iStockphoto, pp. 24, 25; Wikimedia Commons, p. 26 (bottom left); Wilfredo Lee/AP Images, p. 29 (top right)

Populations figures from census.gov

Library of Congress Control Number: 2019943338

Publisher's Cataloging-in-Publication Data
Names: Murray, Julie, author.
Title: Oklahoma / by Julie Murray
Description: Minneapolis, Minnesota : Abdo Publishing, 2020 | Series: Explore the United States | Includes online resources and index.
Identifiers: ISBN 9781532191398 (lib. bdg.) | ISBN 9781532178122 (ebook)
Subjects: LCSH: U.S. states--Juvenile literature. | Southwestern States--Juvenile literature. | Physical geography--United States--Juvenile literature. | Oklahoma--History--Juvenile literature.
Classification: DDC 976.6--dc23

CONTENTS

ONE NATION

The United States is a diverse country. It has farmland, cities, coasts, and mountains. Its people come from many different backgrounds. And, its history covers more than 200 years.

Today the country includes 50 states. Oklahoma is one of these states. Let's learn more about Oklahoma and its story!

DID YOU KNOW?

Oklahoma became a state on November 16, 1907. It was the forty-sixth state to join the nation.

Oklahoma is known for its grassy plains.

CHAPTER 2

OKLAHOMA UP CLOSE

The United States has four main regions. Oklahoma is in the South.

Oklahoma has six states on its borders. Colorado and Kansas are north. Missouri and Arkansas are east. Texas is south and west. New Mexico lies to the west.

Oklahoma has a total area of 69,899 square miles (181,038 sq km). About 3.9 million people live there.

Puerto Rico became a US commonwealth in 1952.

DID YOU KNOW?

Washington, DC, is the US capital city. Puerto Rico is a US commonwealth. This means it is governed by its own people.

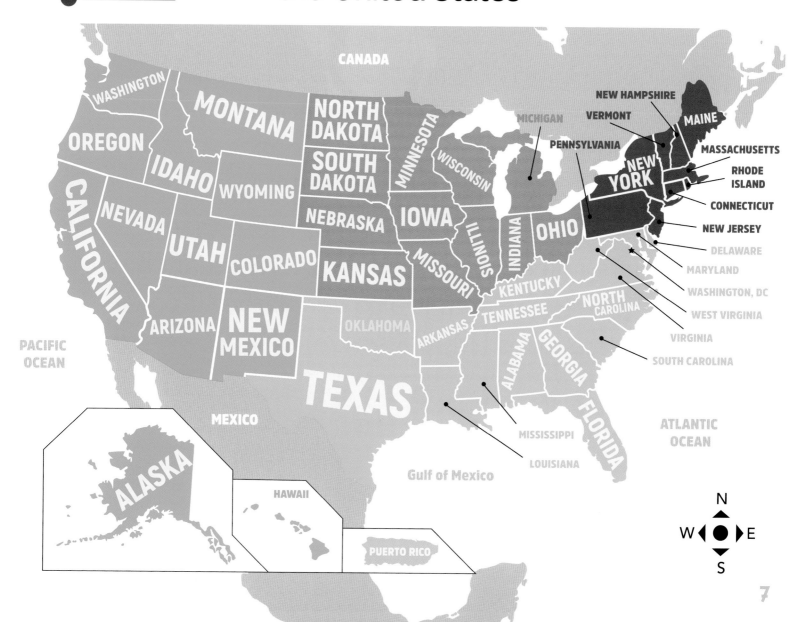

Regions of the United States

West
Midwest
South
Northeast

CANADA

WASHINGTON
OREGON
MONTANA
NORTH DAKOTA
SOUTH DAKOTA
IDAHO
WYOMING
MINNESOTA
WISCONSIN
MICHIGAN
CALIFORNIA
NEVADA
UTAH
COLORADO
NEBRASKA
IOWA
ILLINOIS
INDIANA
OHIO
ARIZONA
NEW MEXICO
KANSAS
MISSOURI
KENTUCKY
TENNESSEE
NORTH CAROLINA
OKLAHOMA
ARKANSAS
ALABAMA
GEORGIA
FLORIDA
TEXAS
MISSISSIPPI
LOUISIANA

NEW HAMPSHIRE
VERMONT
MAINE
PENNSYLVANIA
NEW YORK
MASSACHUSETTS
RHODE ISLAND
CONNECTICUT
NEW JERSEY
DELAWARE
MARYLAND
WASHINGTON, DC
WEST VIRGINIA
VIRGINIA
SOUTH CAROLINA

PACIFIC OCEAN

MEXICO

ALASKA

HAWAII

PUERTO RICO

Gulf of Mexico

ATLANTIC OCEAN

N
W E
S

CHAPTER 3

IMPORTANT CITIES

Oklahoma City is Oklahoma's capital. It is also the state's largest city, with 649,021 people. The city is known for producing oil.

Oklahoma City is also known for its size. It is one of the biggest US cities. It has more than 600 square miles (1,554 sq km) of total area! The city's metropolitan area is also very large. It covers 5,581 square miles (14,445 sq km) of land.

OKLAHOMA CITY The Oklahoma State Capitol is in one of the area's major oil fields. There is an oil well on the grounds.

TULSA

OKLAHOMA CITY

NORMAN

TULSA has many green plants and trees. It looks different from much of Oklahoma, which is drier.

NORMAN is home to the University of Oklahoma.

Norman is near Lake Thunderbird State Park.

Tulsa is Oklahoma's second-largest city, with 400,669 people. The Arkansas River runs through the city. Tulsa is known for producing oil.

Norman is the state's third-largest city. It is home to 123,471 people. This historic city was built around a Santa Fe Railway station.

DID YOU KNOW?
Oklahoma City is home to many large businesses. Sonic Drive-In restaurants are based there.

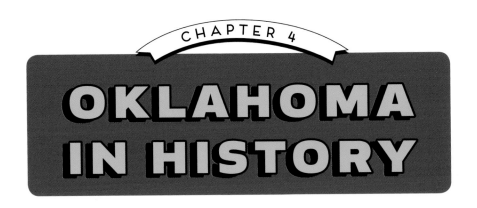

CHAPTER 4

OKLAHOMA IN HISTORY

Oklahoma's history includes Native Americans and settlers. For thousands of years, Native American tribes lived on the land. They hunted, fished, farmed, and gathered wild food.

Beginning in 1830, many Native American tribes were moved to Indian Territory. This was called the Trail of Tears. Indian Territory included part of present-day Oklahoma. In 1889, some of the land was given to white settlers. In 1907, Oklahoma became a state.

DID YOU KNOW?
Some of the new settlers moved to the land before they were supposed to. They were called "sooners." That is why Oklahoma is called the "Sooner State."

In 1889, new settlers lined up and raced to claim land in Oklahoma. This was called a land run.

CHAPTER 5

ACROSS THE LAND

Oklahoma has mountains, plains, lakes, rivers, and forests. The Sandstone Hills, Ouachita (WAH-shuh-taw) Mountains, and Wichita Mountains are in the state. Major rivers include the Red and the Arkansas Rivers.

Many types of animals make their homes in Oklahoma. These include horned toads, water moccasin snakes, and bison.

DID YOU KNOW?

In July, the average high temperature in Oklahoma is 94°F (34.4°C). In January, it is 50.5°F (10.3°C).

Some parts of Oklahoma are grassy and green. Others are dry and have cactus plants.

CHAPTER 6

TORNADO ALLEY

Oklahoma is located in Tornado Alley. This part of the United States is known for having many tornadoes.

A tornado is a spinning, twisting funnel of air. Most tornadoes last for just a few minutes. But, they can last more than an hour.

Tornadoes are very powerful and can tear apart towns. Some have winds as fast as 300 miles (483 km) an hour!

DID YOU KNOW?
Tornado Alley also includes Kansas, Texas, and Nebraska.

Tornadoes are common in the flat, grassy lands of Oklahoma from April to June.

CHAPTER 7

EARNING A LIVING

Oklahoma has important businesses. Many people have jobs with the government or helping visitors to the state. Some work at US Air Force bases. Others work for companies that make food or machinery.

Oklahoma has many natural resources. Oil fields are found on its land. Farms provide wheat, dairy products, cotton, and soybeans. Farmers also raise livestock, such as cattle and pigs.

Oil is one of Oklahoma's most important products. It is removed from the ground at oil wells.

CHAPTER 8

HOMETOWN HEROES

Many famous people are from Oklahoma. Baseball player Mickey Mantle was born in Spavinaw in 1931. From 1951 to 1968, Mantle played for the New York Yankees. He hit 536 home runs during his career! In 1974, he joined the National Baseball Hall of Fame.

Shannon Lucid grew up in Bethany. She became a scientist and astronaut. Lucid went on five space missions in the 1980s and 1990s. Later, she served as NASA's chief scientist.

On her final mission, Lucid spent 188 days in space!

Mantle was called "The Mick."

Alfre Woodard was born in Tulsa in 1952. She is an award-winning actor. She has appeared in plays, movies, and TV shows. Woodard also cofounded a charity that helps poor people in South Africa.

Will Rogers was born in Oologah in 1879. Rogers started out as a cowboy. Later, he appeared in Wild West shows. Over time, he became a famous entertainer in movies and on the radio. Rogers also gave speeches and wrote books and newspaper articles.

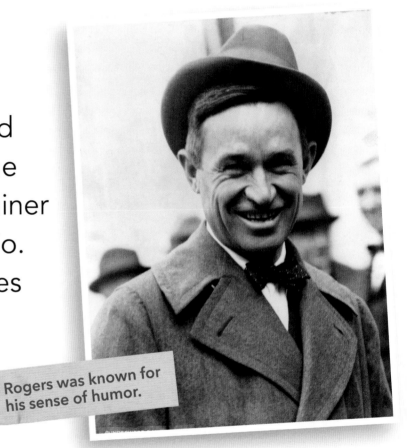

Rogers was known for his sense of humor.

Woodard has also done voice acting. She is the voice of Sarabi in the 2019 movie *The Lion King*.

CHAPTER 9

A GREAT STATE

The story of Oklahoma is important to the United States. The people and places that make up this state offer something special to the country. Together with all the states, Oklahoma helps make the United States great.

The Red River forms nearly all of Oklahoma's southern border with Texas.

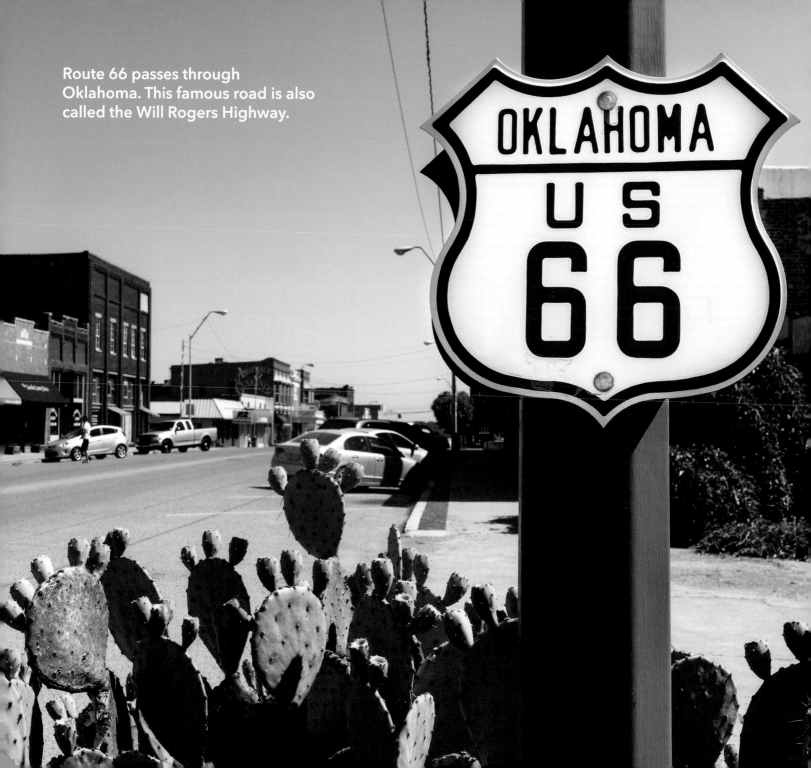

Route 66 passes through Oklahoma. This famous road is also called the Will Rogers Highway.

TIMELINE

1838

Cherokee Native Americans from the southern states were forced to move to the Indian Territory. They faced hunger, sickness, and cold. Thousands died. The move became known as the "Trail of Tears."

1897

The first large oil well was drilled in Bartlesville.

1907

Oklahoma became the forty-sixth state on November 16.

1800s

1900s

President Thomas Jefferson bought land for the United States as part of the **Louisiana Purchase**. The land included present-day Oklahoma.

1803

Settlers claimed land in Oklahoma in a famous land run.

1889

1910

Oklahoma City became the state **capital**.

1928

Oil was discovered in Oklahoma City. This led to a large oil boom in the state.

2011

A set of tornadoes touched down in May. People died and buildings were torn apart throughout the state. One of the tornadoes struck an area 50 miles (80 km) long!

2000s

A **bomb** destroyed the Alfred P. Murrah Federal Building in Oklahoma City. It killed 168 people.

1995

Heavy rainfall in May caused record flooding in parts of Oklahoma and nearby states.

2015

27

TOUR BOOK

Do you want to go to Oklahoma? If you visit the state, here are some places to go and things to do!

EXPLORE
Learn about Route 66, a famous American highway that crosses Oklahoma. There are two Route 66 museums in the state. One is in Clinton and the other is in Elk City (*pictured*).

SEE
Learn about Native Americans at Cherokee Heritage Center near Tahlequah. The center puts on plays and has an ancient village display.

The Heritage Center also has statues of people walking the Trail of Tears.

CHEER

Watch a University of Oklahoma football game! The Sooners have won the conference championship 48 times, including in 2018!

Kyler Murray was a star player for the Sooners. He went on to play in the NFL.

REMEMBER

Visit the Oklahoma City National Memorial. It honors those who died when the Alfred P. Murrah Federal Building was bombed.

LISTEN

Take in some live music at Cain's Ballroom in Tulsa. It was built in 1924 and became known for western swing music.

FAST FACTS

▶ STATE FLOWER
Oklahoma Rose

▶ STATE TREE
Eastern Redbud

▶ STATE BIRD
Scissor-Tailed
Flycatcher

▶ STATE FLAG:

OKLAHOMA

▶ NICKNAME:
Sooner State

▶ DATE OF STATEHOOD:
November 16, 1907

▶ POPULATION (RANK):
3,943,079
(28th most-populated state)

▶ TOTAL AREA (RANK):
69,899 square miles
(20th largest state)

▶ STATE CAPITAL: Oklahoma City

▶ POSTAL ABBREVIATION:
OK

▶ MOTTO:
"Labor Omnia Vincit"
(Labor Conquers All Things)

GLOSSARY

astronaut—a person who is trained for space travel.

bomb (BAHM)—a weapon made to explode when set off.

capital—a city where government leaders meet.

diverse—made up of things that are different from each other.

Louisiana Purchase—land the United States purchased from France in 1803. It extended from the Mississippi River to the Rocky Mountains and from Canada through the Gulf of Mexico.

metropolitan—of or relating to a large city, usually with nearby smaller cities called suburbs.

plains—flat or rolling land without trees.

region—a large part of a country that is different from other parts.

resource—a supply of something useful or valued.

ONLINE RESOURCES

Booklinks
NONFICTION NETWORK
FREE! ONLINE NONFICTION RESOURCES

To learn more about Oklahoma, please visit **abdobooklinks.com** or scan this QR code. These links are routinely monitored and updated to provide the most current information available.

INDEX